Novels for Students, Volume 22

Project Editors: Sara Constantakis and Ira Mark Milne **Editorial**: Anne Marie Hacht

Rights Acquisition and Management: Sue Rudolph, Jessica Schultz, Timothy Sisler **Manufacturing**: Drew Kalasky

Imaging: Leitha Etheridge-Sims, Lezlie Light, Mike Logusz **Product Design**: Pamela A. E. Galbreath **Vendor Administration**: Civie Green

Product Manager: Meggin Condino

© 2006 Gale, a part of Cengage Learning Inc.

Cengage and Burst Logo are trademarks and Gale is a registered trademark used herein under license.

For more information, contact
Gale, an imprint of Cengage Learning
27500 Drake Rd.
Farmington Hills, MI 48331-3535
Or you can visit our Internet site at

http://www.gale.com **ALL RIGHTS RESERVED**

No part of this work covered by the copyright hereon may be reproduced or used in any form or by any means—graphic, electronic, or mechanical, including photocopying, recording, taping, Web distribution, or information storage retrieval systems—without the written permission of the publisher.

For permission to use material from this product, submit your request via Web at http://www.gale-edit.com/permissions, or you may download our Permissions Request form and submit your request by fax or mail to: *Permissions Department*
Gale, an imprint of Cengage Learning
27500 Drake Rd.
Farmington Hills, MI 48331-3535

Permissions Hotline:
248-699-8006 or 800-877-4253, ext. 8006
Fax: 248-699-8074 or 800-762-4058

Since this page cannot legibly accommodate all copyright notices, the acknowledgments constitute an extension of the copyright notice.

While every effort has been made to ensure the reliability of the information presented in this publication, Gale, an imprint of Cengage Learning does not guarantee the accuracy of the data contained herein. Gale, an imprint of Cengage Learning accepts no payment for listing; and inclusion in the publication of any organization, agency, institution, publication, service, or individual does not imply endorsement of the editors or publisher. Errors brought to the attention of the publisher and verified to the satisfaction of the publisher will be corrected in future editions.

ISBN 0-7876-6945-8
ISSN 1094-3552

Printed in the United States of America
10 9 8 7 6 5 4 3 2 1

The God of Small Things

Arundhati Roy 1997

Introduction

Arundhati Roy's debut novel *The God of Small Things* rapidly became a world-renowned literary sensation after it was published in New Delhi in 1997. Immediately recognized as a passionate, sophisticated, and lushly descriptive work, it won Britain's prestigious Booker Prize and launched its author to international fame. The novel tells the story of the Kochammas, a wealthy Christian family in a small village in the southern Indian state of Kerala. Based loosely from the perspective of Rahel Kochamma, who has returned to her hometown to see her twin brother, it pieces together the story of the dramatic events of Rahel's childhood that drastically changed the lives of everyone in the family.

The God of Small Things is an ambitious work that addresses universal themes ranging from religion to biology. Roy stresses throughout the novel that great and small themes are interconnected, and that historical events and seemingly unrelated details have far-reaching consequences throughout a community and country. The novel is therefore able to comment simultaneously on universal, abstract themes, and a wide variety of ideas relating to the personal and family history of the members of the Kochamma family as well as the wider concerns of the Kerala region of India. Some of the novel's most thoroughly developed themes are forbidden love, Indian history, and politics. It is in love and politics that Roy's carefully constructed, multifaceted narrative tends to dwell, and it is when love, politics, and history combine that Roy is able to communicate her most profound authorial insights.

Author Biography

Born circa 1960, Roy grew up in Aymanam, a village in the state of Kerala, in southern India. Her father, a Hindu tea planter from Bengal, was divorced from her Syrian Christian mother when Roy was very young, and Roy was raised by her mother, who ran an informal school. Roy left home when she was sixteen and lived in a squatter's colony in New Delhi, selling empty beer bottles for a living. She eventually went to architectural school and married a fellow student, Gerard Da Cunha. Both quit their studies and moved to Goa, which is in Southwestern India. Roy eventually left Da Cunha and moved back to New Delhi where she found a job at the National Institute of Urban Affairs.

While living in New Delhi, Roy met the film director Pradeep Krishen (whom she later married) and accepted a small acting role that he offered. Soon afterwards, she traveled to Italy on a scholarship to study monument restoration. Roy began to write screenplays while she was in Italy, and she and Krishen later collaborated on a television series that was cancelled after they had shot several episodes. She then wrote two screenplays that became films, and she began to write prose until her critical essay of the celebrated film *Bandit Queen* caused considerable controversy. Roy withdrew to private life to work on her debut novel, which took her nearly five years to complete.

The God of Small Things rapidly became an international sensation, winning Britain's Booker Prize. After its publication, Roy began to work as a political activist, writing essays and giving speeches on a variety of issues, including capitalist globalization, the rights of oppressed groups, and the negative influence of United States culture and governmental policy on the rest of the world. She has been imprisoned for her positions and activism, but she continues to fight for a variety of liberal causes. Roy received the Sydney Peace Prize in November of 2004.

Plot Summary

Chapter 1

The God of Small Things begins with Rahel returning to her childhood home in Ayemenem, India, to see her twin brother Estha, who has been sent to Ayemenem by their father. Events flash back to Rahel and Estha's birth and the period before their mother Ammu divorced their father. Then the narrator describes the funeral of Sophie Mol, Rahel and Estha's cousin, and the point after the funeral when Ammu went to the police station to say that a terrible mistake had been made. Two weeks after this point, Estha was returned to his father.

The narrator briefly describes the twins' adult lives before they return to Ayemenem. In the present, Baby Kochamma gloats that Estha does not speak to Rahel just as he does not speak to anyone else, and then the narrator gives an overview of Baby Kochamma's life. Rahel looks out the window at the building that used to contain the family business, Paradise Pickles and Preserves, and flashes back to the circumstances surrounding Sophie Mol's death.

Chapters 2–4

The second chapter describes the trip in which Rahel, Estha, Ammu, Chacko, and Baby

Kochamma travel to the town of Cochin in order to pick up Margaret Kochamma and Sophie Mol from the airport. They are on the way to see *The Sound of Music*, but they are delayed at a train crossing by a Marxist demonstration in which Rahel sees her friend Velutha, who is a Paravan, or Untouchable Hindu, employed by the Kochamma family. When she yells to him out the window, Ammu scolds her furiously.

A flashback describes Velutha and his relations with the Kochamma family, and then one of the protesters opens Rahel's door and makes Baby Kochamma wave a Marxist flag. Before they drive away, Chacko says that Ammu, Estha, and Rahel are "millstones around his neck." In chapter 3, which takes place in the present day, the narrator describes the filthiness of the Ayemenem House. Estha comes home, goes upstairs, and takes off his clothes to wash them while Rahel watches.

Chapter 4 continues the story of the family trip at the point when they arrive at the movie theater. Ammu makes Estha go to the lobby because he cannot resist singing along, and the Orangedrink Lemondrink Man at the refreshments counter forces Estha to masturbate him. The family leaves early because Ammu sees that Estha will be sick, and on the way out she comments on the sweetness of the Orangedrink Lemondrink Man. Rahel says "why don't you marry him, then?" Ammu tells her that comments like these make people love you a little less. Rahel worries that Ammu will love Sophie Mol more than her. The twins fall asleep next to each other in Chacko's room.

Chapters 5–7

Back in the present day, the narrator describes the filthiness of the river, just a stream now because of a saltwater barrage, and the five-star hotel that has taken over the "History House," which was formerly the home of an Englishman who took on traditional Indian customs. Rahel then answers Comrade Pillai's invasive questions and remembers his son Lenin.

In chapter 6, the family picks up Margaret and Sophie Mol from the Cochin Airport. Baby Kochamma tells the twins they are the ambassadors of India. Chacko happily introduces everyone, but Estha does not say "How do YOU do?" as Ammu requests, and Rahel hides behind a curtain. Ammu later scolds them angrily, and the twins talk with Sophie Mol.

Chapter 7 is in the present day, when Rahel finds her and Estha's "*Wisdom Exercise Notebooks*" and reads the corrections that Ammu made in them. She remembers Ammu's last visit before she died and the lonely circumstances of her mother's death.

Chapters 8–11

When the family arrives at the Ayemenem House with Margaret and Sophie Mol, the narrator compares the situation to a play. Rahel escapes from the distribution of Sophie Mol's cake to play with

Velutha, and Ammu exchanges a meaningful glance with Velutha.

In chapter 9, Rahel remembers her and Estha becoming friends with Sophie Mol, and, in the present day, she walks into the abandoned factory. Chapter 10 describes Estha's thoughts while he wandered from Sophie Mol's reception at the house and into the pickle factory. He and Rahel decide to take a stockpile of things to the History House. The twins find a boat by the river and Velutha helps them repair it. In chapter 11, Ammu dreams of a one-armed man until the twins wake her, and she realizes that Velutha is the man of whom she dreamed, the God of Small Things.

Chapters 12–15

In the present day, Rahel goes to see the traditional kathakali dancing in the Ayemenem temple and Estha shows up as well. Chapter 13 recalls the story of Margaret and Chacko's relationship and then describes the circumstances leading up to Sophie Mol's drowning, beginning with Vellya Paapen's visit to the Ayemenem House. Vellya Paapen tells Mammachi of Velutha's affair with Ammu and offers to kill his son, and Mammachi shouts, spits at him, and pushes him to the ground. Mammachi and Baby Kochamma then manage to lock Ammu in her room, and the next morning they receive the news that a white child was found drowned in the river.

At the police station, Baby Kochamma lies to

Inspector Thomas Mathew that Velutha threatened them and tried to force himself on Ammu. The inspector then interviews Comrade Pillai about whether Velutha has any political support and, discovering that he does not, instructs his men to attack Velutha.

In chapter 14, Chacko visits Comrade Pillai and asks him about Velutha. Comrade Pillai, because of his own ambitions in the Communist Party, tells Chacko that Velutha is a dangerous party member who should be fired. Velutha comes to see Comrade Pillai, after Mammachi screams at him and fires him, and Comrade Pillai tells Velutha that he has no support from the party. In chapter 15, Velutha swims across the river to the History House.

Chapters 16–20

The twins and Sophie Mol run away from home in chapter 16, and Sophie Mol drowns after their boat tips over on the way to the History House. Chapter 17, in the present day, describes Rahel and Estha lying in bed, remembering their childhood. In chapter 18, the Kottayam police find Velutha sleeping next to Rahel and Estha at the History House, they and beat him until he is nearly dead.

Inspector Mathew interviews the twins in chapter 19 and discovers that Velutha is innocent. He tells Baby Kochamma that if the children do not identify Velutha as their abductor, he will accuse Baby Kochamma of filing a false report. Baby

Kochamma tells the twins that they and Ammu will go to jail unless they accuse Velutha, and Estha goes into Velutha's cell to condemn him. It is not until the next morning, after Velutha has died, that Ammu goes to the police station to set the record straight.

Chapter 20 describes the scene at the train station when Estha is leaving for Calcutta, and then changes to the present tense, when Estha and Rahel begin to make love. Chapter 21 flashes back to the point at which Ammu finds Velutha at the river and she and Velutha make love for the first time.

Characters

Aleyooty Ammachi

Aleyooty Ammachi is Rahel and Estha's great-grandmother. Her portrait hangs prominently beside that of Reverend Ipe in the Ayemenem House.

Baba

Baba is Estha and Rahel's father. Ammu divorces him when the children are very young. He was a violent alcoholic who not only beat his wife and children, but attempted to prostitute his wife to his English employer. Baba has remarried, resigned from his job on a tea plantation, and "more or less" stopped drinking when, after Sophie Mol's death, Estha moves in with him in Calcutta. When Estha is an adult, Baba sends him back to Ayemenem and emigrates to Australia.

Reverend E. John Ipe

Estha and Rahel's great-grandfather, Reverend Ipe had been known as Punnyan Kunju, or "Little Blessed One," since he was blessed by the Syrian Christian Patriarch at age seven.

Joe

Joe is Margaret Kochamma's second husband, who dies in a car accident shortly before Margaret and Sophie Mol travel to Ayemenem.

The Kathakali Men

Karna and Kunti, the Kathakali Men, perform the traditional Hindu dancing that Rahel and Estha go to see.

Ammu Kochamma

Ammu is Rahel and Estha's mother. She is a beautiful and sardonic woman who has been victimized first by her father and then her husband. While raising her children, she has become tense and repressed. Ammu grew up in Delhi but, because her father said that college was an unnecessary expense for a girl, was forced to live with her parents when they moved to Ayemenem. She met her future husband at a wedding reception. She later divorces him and returns to the Ayemenem House when he starts to abuse the twins.

Ammu's latent "Unsafe Edge," full of desire and "reckless rage," emerges during Sophie Mol's visit and draws her to Velutha. After the horrific climax to the affair, Ammu sends Estha to live with his father and leaves Rahel in the Ayemenem House while Ammu looks for work; but Ammu loses a succession of jobs because she is ill. Ammu dies alone in a cheap hotel at the age of thirty-one. Chacko has her cremated because the Syrian

Christian Church will not bury her.

Baby Kochamma

Nicknamed "Baby," Mammachi's sister, Navomi Ipe Kochamma, is a judgmental old maid with tiny feet. Rahel thinks, "She's living her life backwards," because Baby Kochamma renounces the material world when she is young, but becomes very materialistic when she is old. Throughout her life, Baby Kochamma is an insecure, selfish, and vindictive person.

When she was a girl, Baby Kochamma fell in love with a handsome Irish monk named Father Mulligan who made weekly visits to her father. Although they did nothing more than flirt while talking about the Bible, when he moved to Madras she became a Roman Catholic and entered a convent in Madras in the hopes of being with him. After her hopes were crushed, she left the convent and traveled to the United States to study, returning to India obese and devoted to gardening. During the time of Sophie Mol's visit, Baby Kochamma is a nuisance who pesters the twins because she dislikes them and Ammu. She is later revealed to be cruel and insidious, because she is the one that convinces the twins to condemn Velutha; and it was due to her manipulations of Chacko that Ammu is forced to leave the house and Estha is returned to his father. In her old age, Baby Kochamma becomes a bitter and lonely woman addicted to television, after having locked herself inside the family house.

Chacko Kochamma

Chacko is Ammu's intellectual and self-absorbed older brother. He was a charming but very unclean Rhodes Scholar at Oxford, and he met Margaret while she was working in an Oxford café. Deeply in love with Margaret, in part because she never depended on him or adored him like a mother, he marries her without telling his family. She grows tired of his squalor within a year, however, and divorces him around the time that their daughter is born.

Between his divorce and Sophie Mol's death, Chacko grew fatter and became obsessed with balsawood airplanes, which he unsuccessfully attempted to fly. He was also unsuccessful at running the pickle factory, which started to lose money as soon as he attempted to expand the operation. A "self-proclaimed Marxist," Chacko attempts to be a benevolent employer and even plans to organize a union among his own workers. However, he is insistent that he is the sole owner of his factory, his house, and other possessions that he actually shares with women. Sophie Mol's death is completely devastating for him. After her death, he emigrates to Canada.

Estha Kochamma

Estha, which is short for Esthappen Yako, is Rahel's twin brother. He is a serious, intelligent, and somewhat nervous child who wears "beige and pointy shoes" and has an "Elvis puff." His experience of the circumstances surrounding Sophie Mol's visit is somewhat more traumatic than Rahel's, beginning when he is sexually abused by the Orangdrink Lemondrink Man at the Abhilash Talkies theater. The narrator stresses that Estha's "Two Thoughts" in the pickle factory, which stem from this experience (that "*Anything can happen to Anyone*" and "*It's best to be prepared*") are critical in leading to his cousin's death.

Estha is the twin chosen by Baby Kochamma, because he is more "practical" and "responsible," to go into Velutha's cell and condemn him as their abductor. This trauma, in addition to being shipped to Calcutta to live with his father, contributes to Estha becoming mute at some point in his childhood. Estha never went to college and acquired a number of habits, such as wandering on very long walks and obsessively cleaning his clothes. He is so close to his sister that the narrator describes them as one person, despite having been separated for most of their lives.

Mammachi Kochamma

An elegant woman in her old age although she is nearly blind, Mammachi is Rahel and Estha's grandmother. Brutally beaten by her husband, she nevertheless cries at his funeral and shares many of his values, including an extremely rigid view of the caste system. She began the pickle factory and ran it successfully, and she was an "exceptionally talented" violinist, although Pappachi disallowed her to take further lessons when he heard this. Mammachi loves Chacko with blind admiration and deeply dislikes Margaret Kochamma. Nevertheless, she tolerates and even facilitates Chacko's affairs with factory workers, although she is so horrified when she hears of Ammu's affair with Velutha that she attacks both Velutha and his father, and locks Ammu in her room.

Margaret Kochamma

Margaret is Sophie Mol's mother and Chacko's ex-wife. She is from a strict, working-class London family and was working as a waitress in Oxford when she met Chacko. Marrying him because of his uncontrolled personality that made her feel free, Margaret soon realized that she did not need him to accept herself, and she divorced him. When her second husband Joe dies, Margaret accepts Chacko's invitation to Ayemenem for Christmas, and she is haunted by this decision for the rest of her life. When Margaret sees her daughter's body, she feels an irrational rage towards the twins and seeks out Estha several times to slap him.

Pappachi Kochamma

Shri Benaan John Ipe, known in the family as Pappachi, is Rahel and Estha's grandfather. He was an "Imperial Entomologist" under British rule and an Anglophile whose greatest setback was not having named a moth that he discovered because government scientists failed to recognize it as a new species until later. Seventeen years older than his wife, he was extremely resentful of her and beat her regularly with a brass vase until Chacko ordered him never to do it again. Pappachi Kochamma also beat his daughter and smashed furniture, although in public he convinced everyone that he was compassionate and neglected by his wife. In his old age, he rode around in his blue Plymouth that he kept entirely to himself.

Rahel Kochamma

Rahel is Ammu's daughter and Estha's younger sister by eighteen minutes. An intelligent and honest person who has never felt socially comfortable, she is something of a drifter, and several times the narrator refers to her as the quality "Emptiness." When she is a girl, her hair sits "on top of her head like a fountain" and she always wears red-tinted plastic sunglasses with yellow rims.

Although Ammu often chastises Rahel for being dirty and unsafe, she loves her very deeply, and Rahel is equally devoted to her mother. Rahel also loves Velutha and her brother, with whom she shares a "single Siamese soul." She is traumatized by Sophie Mol's drowning, Velutha's death, and Ammu's death. Although these events do not seem to deprive her of her quirkiness or brightness, they contribute to her sense of sadness and lack of direction in later life. After Ammu dies, Rahel drifts between schools, receiving little attention from Mammachi or Chacko. Rahel then enters an architecture school but never finishes the course, marries an American named Larry McCaslin, and lives with him in Boston until they are divorced. She moves to Washington, D.C. and spends several years as a night clerk at a gas station before returning to Ayemenem to see Estha.

Kochu Maria

Kochu Maria is the Kochamma family's "vinegar-hearted, short-tempered, midget cook." She does not speak any English and, although she has always "noticed everything," she eventually stops caring about how the house looks and becomes addicted to television.

Kochu Thomban

Kochu Thomban is the Ayemenem temple elephant. When Rahel sees him in the present day, he is no longer "Kochu Thomban" ("Little Tusker") but "Vellya Thomban" ("Big Tusker").

Kuttappen

Velutha's older brother, Kuttappen is paralyzed from the chest down and confined to his house, which he shares with his brother and father.

Inspector Thomas Mathew

The Kottayam police chief is a practical, cynical, and brutal man who deals carefully with the scandal of Sophie Mol's death and Ammu's affair with Velutha. He taps on Ammu's breasts and insults her when she comes to make a statement about Velutha because the police chief strongly believes in the conventional caste system.

Larry McCaslin

Larry is Rahel's American husband, whom she met at the college of architecture in Delhi while he was working on a doctoral thesis, and with whom she moves to Boston. He holds her "as though she was a gift" and notices a hollowness in Rahel's eyes that seems to contribute to their lack of understanding and eventual divorce.

Miss Mitten

Rahel and Estha's tutor whom they dislike, Miss Mitten is a Born Again Christian who scolds the twins for reading backwards. She is killed by a milk van.

Father Mulligan

Father Mulligan was Baby Kochamma's would-be lover. An Irish monk who came to Kerala to study Hindu scriptures "in order to be able to denounce them intelligently," he flirted with Baby Kochamma while ostensibly talking about the Bible. Eventually, he converts to Hinduism, staying in touch with Baby Kochamma, and dies of viral hepatitis.

Murlidharan

Perched on the milestone of an intersection, Murlidharan is the "level-crossing lunatic" the family encounters on their way to Cochin.

Comrade E. M. S. Namboodiripad

Chacko's hero and the leader of Kerala's democratically elected Communist government, Comrade Namboodiripad is a moderate, particularly during his second term.

Orangedrink Lemondrink Man

The man who works behind the refreshments counter at the Abhilash Talkies movie theater forces Estha to masturbate him. He looks like an "unfriendly jeweled bear" and deeply traumatizes Estha, who believes the Orangedrink Lemondrink Man will find him in Ayemenem.

Comrade K. N. M. Pillai

Comrade Pillai is "essentially a political man" who plots to become the leader of the Communist Party in Ayemenem. With many connections and building influence, he is involved in a number of business ventures, including making signs for the pickle factory. After he betrays Velutha because he wants to rid himself of any competition in the party ranks, Comrade Pillai lays the seeds for dissatisfaction among the workers of Paradise Pickles and organizes the unionization that contributes to the factory's collapse. This does not help him rise to power in the party, however.

Kalyani Pillai

Kalyani is Comrade Pillai's quiet wife.

Latha Pillai

Comrade Pillai's niece, Latha, recites a poem by Sir Walter Scott for Chacko.

Lenin Pillai

Lenin is Comrade Pillai's son. He is a slightly awkward boy who grows up to be a secretary in Delhi.

Kari Saipu

Kari Saipu is the "Black Sahib," the Englishman who took on traditional Indian customs. The twins know his house, which was unoccupied after Kari Saipu shot himself, as "the History House." This house is the location of Ammu and Velutha's meetings.

Sophie Mol

Sophie Mol is Chacko and Margaret's daughter. She is a frank and spirited English girl characterized by her bellbottoms and her go-go bag. Although the twins are prejudiced against her because they have been so insistently instructed about how to behave when she arrives, she manages to win them over. This is partly because she is charming and outgoing, and partly because she rejected the advances of Chacko, Mammachi, and Baby Kochamma in favor of befriending Rahel and Estha.

One reason Sophie Mol's death is so important to the book's main themes is that she represents a combination of Indian and British identities. The narrator is careful to call her "Sophie," her English name, combined with "Mol," the phrase for "girl" in the local language of Malayalam. Although Sophie Mol never takes to Indian culture, she does make a great effort with the twins before she accidentally falls into the river and drowns.

Vellya Paapen

Velutha's father, Vellya is an "Old-World Paravan" who feels he is indebted to Mammachi for paying for his glass eye. He is tortured about his son's affair with Ammu and tells Mammachi about it.

Velutha

An Untouchable worker at the pickle factory

and a close friend to Rahel and Estha, Velutha is blamed for killing Sophie Mol and raping Ammu. In fact, he has nothing to do with Sophie Mol's death, and he carries on a brief and voluntary affair with Ammu until Inspector Thomas Mathew's police officers beat Velutha until he is nearly dead.

Velutha's name means "White" in Malayalam, so-called because he has such dark skin. Mammachi noticed his prodigious talents in making and fixing things when he was young and convinced his father to send him to the Untouchables' School founded by her father-in-law. Velutha became an accomplished carpenter and mechanic, and acquired an assurance that scared his father because it was unacceptable among Untouchables. Velutha disappeared for four years and was hired by Mammachi upon his return to Ayemenem. A member of the Communist Party, he never quite fits into his role as an Untouchable, and he begins an extremely passionate affair with Ammu when Sophie Mol arrives in Ayemenem. After Comrade Pillai refuses to help him, the police officers beat him, and Estha identifies him as their abductor. Velutha dies in jail.

Themes

Indian History and Politics

Indian history and politics shape the plot and meaning of *The God of Small Things* in a variety of ways. Some of Roy's commentary is on the surface, with jokes and snippets of wisdom about political realities in India. However, the novel also examines the historical roots of these realities and develops profound insights into the ways in which human desperation and desire emerge from the confines of a firmly entrenched caste society. Roy reveals a complex and longstanding class conflict in the state of Kerala, India, and she comments on its various competing forces.

For example, Roy's novel attacks the brutal, entrenched, and systematic oppression at work in Kerala, exemplified by figures of power such as Inspector Thomas Mathew. Roy is also highly critical of the hypocrisy and ruthlessness of the conventional, traditional moral code of Pappachi and Mammachi. On the opposite side of the political fence, the Kerala Communist Party, at least the faction represented by Comrade Pillai, is revealed to be much more concerned with personal ambition than with any notions of social justice.

Class Relations and Cultural

Tensions

In addition to her commentary on Indian history and politics, Roy evaluates the Indian postcolonial complex, or the cultural attitudes of many Indians towards their former British rulers. After Ammu calls her father a "[sh——t]-wiper" in Hindi for his blind devotion to the British, Chacko explains to the twins that they come from a family of Anglophiles, or lovers of British culture, "trapped outside their own history and unable to retrace their steps," and he goes on to say that they despise themselves because of this.

Topics for Further Study

- Roy has published a great deal of political writing, has worked as an activist, and has been imprisoned for her political beliefs. Research her political views and activities, and read some of her political writings. How would you characterize Roy's position on issues such as globalization and terrorism? What have been the results of her activism in India and around the world?

- As an Indian novel written in English, *The God of Small Things* is part of a genre of literature stretching back to the days of the British Raj. Research the ways in which Roy's novel relates to this tradition, which includes authors such as R. K. Narayan and Salman Rushdie. In what ways does Roy's novel fit into this tradition, and in what ways does it belong outside of it? What innovations does Roy bring to Indian literature in English, and why are they important? How does Roy's novel relate to Indian politics, and how is this similar or different to the ways in which the novels of her predecessors have related to Indian politics?

- Some readers and critics have found elements of *The God of Small Things* offensive or controversial. Research the nature of the outcry against the novel, particularly in India and in Britain. Which aspects of the work were controversial, and why? What were the results of the controversy? Describe your reaction to moments of the novel such as when Estha is forced to masturbate the Orangedrink Lemondrink Man, when Ammu and Velutha make love, and when Rahel and Estha make love. Discuss how elements of the forbidden and the taboo relate to the central themes of the novel.

- Communism has been a uniquely prominent force in the state of Kerala, India. Research the activities of the various factions of the Communist Party in Kerala. How did communism develop and spread in the region? What are the key ways in which communist thought has affected Kerala's history? How does the history of the communist parties in Kerala relate to the history of communism throughout South Asia? Discuss the state of communism in Kerala today.

A related inferiority complex is evident in the interactions between Untouchables and Touchables in Ayemenem. Vellya Paapen is an example of an Untouchable so grateful to the Touchable class that he is willing to kill his son when he discovers that his son has broken the most important rule of class segregation—that there be no inter-class sexual relations. Nearly all of the relationships in the novel are somehow colored by cultural and class tension, including the twins' relationship with Sophie Mol, Chacko's relationship with Margaret, Pappachi's relationship with his family, and Ammu's relationship with Velutha. Characters such as Baby Kochamma and Pappachi are the most rigid and vicious in their attempts to uphold that social code, while Ammu and Velutha are the most unconventional and daring in unraveling it. Roy implies that this is why they are punished so severely for their transgression.

Forbidden Love

The many types of love in Roy's novel, whether they are described as erotic, familial, incestuous, biological, or hopeless, are important to the novel's meaning. However, Roy focuses her authorial commentary on forbidden and taboo types of love, including Ammu's love for Velutha and Rahel's love for Estha. Both relationships are rigidly forbidden by what Roy calls the "Love Laws," or "The laws that lay down who should be loved, and how. / And how much." Although breaking these laws is the worst of taboos, and those who break them are brutally punished, desire and desperation overcome the Love Laws at the key moments of Roy's novel.

One interpretation of Roy's theme of forbidden love is that love is such a powerful and uncontrollable force that it cannot be contained by any conventional social code. Another is that conventional society somehow seeks to destroy real love, which is why love in the novel is consistently connected to loss, death, and sadness. Also, because all romantic love in the novel relates closely to politics and history, it is possible that Roy is stressing the interconnectedness of personal desire to larger themes of history and social circumstances. Love would therefore be an emotion that can be explained only in terms of two peoples' cultural backgrounds and political identities.

Style

Non-sequential Narrative

The God of Small Things is not written in a sequential narrative style in which events unfold chronologically. Instead, the novel is a patchwork of flashbacks and lengthy sidetracks that weave together to tell the story of the Kochamma family. The main events of the novel are traced back through the complex history of their causes, and memories are revealed as they relate to each other thematically and as they might appear in Rahel's mind. Although the narrative voice is omniscient, or all-knowing, it is loosely grounded in Rahel's perspective, and all of the episodes of the novel progress towards the key moments in Rahel's life.

This non-sequential narrative style, which determines the form of the novel, is an extremely useful authorial tool. It allows Roy a great deal of flexibility as she chooses which themes and events are most important to pursue. The author is able to structure her book so as to build up to the ideas and events at the root of the Kochamma family's experience.

Foreshadowing

Throughout Roy's novel, the narrative voice emphasizes that it is building towards a mysterious, cataclysmic, and all-important event. Roy even provides details and glimpses of the event, which she refers to as "The Loss of Sophie Mol," and quotes characters remembering it and referring to it vaguely far before the reader discovers what has happened. Because of this technique, called foreshadowing, Roy builds considerable tension and intrigue into *The God of Small Things*, and she is able to play with the expectation and anticipation that the reader feels.

Historical Context

Because of the efforts of the political and religious leader Mohandas Gandhi, India became independent on August 15, 1947 at the stroke of midnight, after more than three hundred years of a British colonial presence. The British partitioned the former colony into the nations of India and Pakistan (comprised of East and West regions), but this was unsuccessful in quelling agitations between Hindus and Muslims. The borders were only rough designations of religious majorities, and millions died as Hindus in Pakistan moved to majority-Hindu India, and Muslims in India moved to majority-Muslim Pakistan. Ammu was five years old in 1947, living with her family in the Indian capital of New Delhi.

Jawaharlal Nehru, the Prime Minister of India from Independence until his death in 1964, struggled to foster economic growth and became involved in various territorial disputes. In Kerala, the Communist Party of India (CPI) was elected to power in a state government led by E. M. S. Namboodiripad in 1957, but Nehru dissolved it in 1959. In 1962, the year Rahel and Estha were born, India fought a limited war over a border dispute with China. As a result of the Chinese conflict, the CPI split between a pro-Russian faction, still called the CPI, and a faction that grew to be less influenced by foreign governments, called the Communist Party of India (Marxist). In the mid-

1960s, a further split in the Indian communist parties formed the Naxalites, who advocated an immediate communist revolution, while tensions between Pakistan and India flared into war in 1965.

After Prime Minister Lal Bahadur Shastri died of a heart attack in 1966, Nehru's daughter Indira Gandhi (no relation to Mohandas Gandhi) assumed the post amidst a severe draught and growing unemployment. These conditions contributed to the major losses that Gandhi's Indian National Congress Party suffered in the 1967 elections. As Gandhi's intentions for the Congress Party became clear, tensions arose between liberal and conservative members of the party, and in 1969, the year of Sophie Mol's visit to Ayemenem, the Congress Party split. Although Indira Gandhi remained in control of the larger, liberal faction, she was forced to forge alliances with left-wing parties in order to maintain control of the government.

Compare & Contrast

- **1969:** E. M. S. Namboodiripad's communist government of Kerala falls for the second time, and the Indian National Congress Party dissolves into two groups.
  1990s: Indian Prime Minister Rajiv Gandhi is assassinated in 1991 and is succeeded by P. V. Narasimha Rao. A series of leadership struggles begins in 1996, when Rao is forced

out of power.

Today: Manmohan Singh is appointed prime minister of India in May of 2004, after the Congress Party unexpectedly wins the election and its leader Sonia Gandhi, widow of Rajiv Gandhi, declines the post in order to appease Hindu nationalists. Communism remains a powerful force in Kerala politics.

- **1969:** Kerala is a lush and warm region of southern India with a uniquely high literacy rate. Public welfare systems have become much more substantial since independence, but the agricultural economy remains similar to the economy in the days of the British Raj.

  1990s: Kerala's economy is still based on rubber, coconut, and spice production, but economic reforms are placing much more emphasis on large private corporations, and India is opening up to foreign investment.

  Today: India has one of the largest and fastest growing economies in the world, and the trend towards privatization continues. Kerala has a literacy rate near ninety percent, which is the highest of any state in India.

- **1969:** Post-colonial Indian literature written in English is becoming a popular genre of its own, developed by writers such as R. K. Narayan.
  1990s: Salman Rushdie has been a dominant force in the Indo-British literary scene since he published *Midnight's Children* in 1981.
  Today: Indian writing in English is a wide and diverse genre of literature, and Roy is one of its most successful stars, even though she has published only one novel.

Further tensions with Pakistan led to India's involvement in a conflict between East Pakistan and West Pakistan in 1971, which led to the independence of Bangladesh (formerly East Pakistan). Indira Gandhi was convicted of minor election law violations in 1975, but she declared a state of emergency in order to stay in power. Widely unpopular, this move allowed her to arrest opposition leaders and censor the press, and she was defeated in the 1977 elections. Gandhi was elected once again in 1980, however, and began to meet with foreign leaders while dealing with several insurgencies in India. In 1984, she sent Indian troops to storm a Sikh temple, killing the Sikh guerillas inside, and this event led to her assassination by two of her Sikh bodyguards. Gandhi's son, Rajiv, succeeded her to the leadership of the Congress Party and was elected prime minister in 1985. Rajiv Gandhi sponsored economic reforms, but he was criticized as an indecisive leader and lost the 1989 election.

Roy wrote her novel in the early 1990s, during a period in which Rajiv Gandhi was assassinated by a Sri Lankan Tamil in 1991 while campaigning for an election that political analysts believe he would have won. The present-day events in *The God of Small Things* occur in 1992, when Congress/I (formerly the Congress Party) leader P. V. Narasimha Rao was prime minister. Rao became known for his sensitive handling of Hindu-Muslim tensions, his economic reforms, and his progressive foreign policy in response to the collapse of the Soviet Union. He lost power in 1996 amidst charges of corruption, however, and this began a series of leadership struggles that continued through India's announcement in 1998 that it was a nuclear power; Pakistan made a similar announcement shortly thereafter.

Critical Overview

The God of Small Things was an unprecedented international success for a first-time author. It won a publishing advance reputed to be near one million dollars, and it won Britain's most prestigious writing award, the Booker Prize, in 1997. Reviews in the United States were very positive, often including high praise such as that of Ritu Menon in her review for *Women's Review of Books*: "*The God of Small Things* is a seduction from start to finish." Although the novel was generally well-reviewed in Britain, there was some controversy about its success, and a minority of critics, including the previous Booker Prize Committee Chairperson Carmen Callil, said on television that it did not deserve the prize. The novel has also caused some controversy in India, where it was first published. Communists, including E. M. S. Namboodiripad, took exception to Roy's portrayal of communist characters, and the lawyer Sabu Thomas filed a public interest petition claiming that the novel was obscene.

Critics generally group the novel into the genre of post-colonial Indian literature that takes Indian politics and history as its subject. For example, the anonymous reviewer in the March 15, 1997 edition of *Kirkus Reviews* characterizes Roy's style as "reminiscent of Salman Rushdie's early work." Like the novels of the influential Indian-British author Salman Rushdie, *The God of Small Things* is written in English, for a Western readership as much as an Indian readership, and it takes on a variety of historical and political themes.

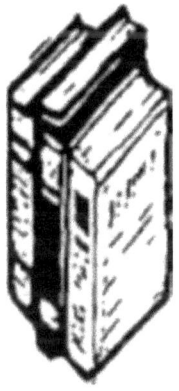

What Do I Read Next?

- *The Guide* (1958) is R. K. Narayan's popular tale of Raju, a former convict who is mistaken for a holy man upon his arrival in Narayan's fictional universe of Malgudi.

- Salman Rushdie's *Midnight's Children* (1981) is a multifaceted and ambitious work about India's history since its independence from Britain. Focusing on the story of Saleem Sinai, who was born at the stroke of midnight marking Independence, it includes elements of magic and fantasy, and it is highly allusive to classic texts including the

Bible and *Arabian Nights*.

- Roy's third volume of nonfiction, *War Talk* (2003), is composed of fluent and engaging arguments about the negative impacts of globalization, the danger of nuclear proliferation, and the devastating impact of the Bush administration's foreign policy on the Third World.

- E. M. Forster's *A Passage to India* (1924) is the classic modernist text about the clash of British and Indian cultures during the British Raj. The plot centers around the Indian Dr. Aziz, who is accused of raping an English woman.

Sources

Menon, Ritu, "The Age of Innocence," in *Women's Review of Books*, Vol. 14, No. 12, September 1997, pp. 1–3.

National University of Singapore, *Postcolonial and Post Imperial Literature online*, www.postcolonialweb.org, March 29, 2005.

Review of *The God of Small Things*, in *Kirkus Reviews*, March 15, 1997, p. 412.

Roy, Arundhati, *The God of Small Things*, Random House, 1997.

Further Reading

Dodiya, Jaydipsinh, and Joya Chakravarty, *The Critical Studies of Arundhati Roy's "The God of Small Things,"* Atlantic Publishers & Distributors, 1999.

> This collection, published in New Delhi, is the earliest book-length volume of criticism on Roy's novel.

Eder, Richard, "As the World Turns," in *Los Angeles Times Book Review*, June 1, 1997, p. 2.

> Eder provides a mixed review of Roy's novel, praising her evocative depiction of the story and characters but arguing that she loses control over the narrative.

Thornmann, Janet, "The Ethical Subject of *The God of Small Things*," in *Journal for the Psychoanalysis of Culture and Society*, Vol. 8, No. 2, Fall 2003, pp. 299–307.

> Thornmann's psychoanalytical interpretation of Roy's novel includes an argument about the applicability of the Oedipal complex to the work.

Truax, Alice, "A Silver Thimble in Her Fist," in the *New York Times Book Review*, May 25, 1997, p. 5.

> Truax's descriptive review of *The*

God of Small Things is an example of the very positive response to Roy's work in the United States.